W9-CAA-441

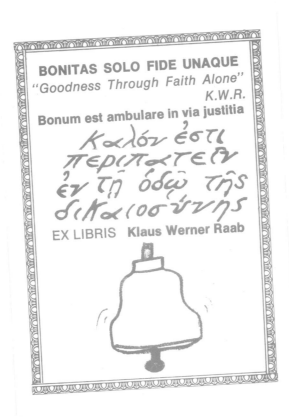

BONITAS SOLO FIDE UNAQUE
"Goodness Through Faith Alone"
K.W.R.

Bonum est ambulare in via justitia

Καλόν ἐστι
περιπατεῖν
ἐν τῇ ὁδῷ τῆς
δικαιοσύνης

EX LIBRIS   **Klaus Werner Raab**

JAPAN IN TRANSITION

One Hundred Years of Modernization

Ministry of Foreign Affairs, Japan

1973

CONTENTS

Japan In Transition

CHAPTER ONE

A Century of Change

THE past century has indeed been one of great change for Japan. When Japan re-opened its doors to the outside world in the middle of the 19th century, it was stagnating under a feudal system which had divided society into four distinct castes: warriors, farmers, artisans and tradesmen. So all pervasive was this caste system that it exercised control over the very lives of the people to the extent of prescribing exact rules on all activities relating to daily life and behaviour. Even the use of language, both written and oral, was determined by the individual's respective social class. The Confucian ethic constituted the foundation on which all relations between superiors and inferiors, one's obedience to authority, and the concept of master-servant were formalized. Society was stable, but thoroughly immobilized.

In 1856, when Townsend Harris arrived in Japan as the first Consul General of the United States, he described in his diary the condition of Japanese society as one where the proverb 'move not that which is still' was being faithfully observed.

Japan of those days, moreover, was an impoverished,

agrarian state. Even in the late 1870's, of the employed population, some 75 per cent to 80 per cent were engaged in agriculture and approximately 65 per cent of the national income was derived from the agricultural sector. Per capita output was estimated at around $65. This means that before Japan embarked upon its rapid economic growth, it was a country sustained by a farming community working at a bare subsistence level.

In the century that followed, Japan underwent a major transformation. From the stagnating society of the mid-nineteenth century described by Townsend Harris, it has become the world's most rapidly changing society. In 1962, *The Economist,* in a special supplement, sought to explore the secret of what it called 'the most exciting and extraordinary sudden forward leaps.' This would seem to reflect the feeling of amazement among the peoples of Europe.

Agrarian State to Industrial Power

Moreover, Japan in the mid-twentieth century is no longer an agrarian state, but rather a major industrial nation which, far from being content with mere subsistence standards of living, is beginning to enjoy those associated with the mass consumption age.

The agricultural population has decreased to less than 20 per cent and per capita national income is about to exceed the $1,000 level. Many experts are predicting that this trend will continue in the future. For example, Herman Kahn, Director of the Hudson Institute in the United States, says the Japanese 'may have the most achievement-oriented culture in history.' He observes that Japan's goal for the past one hundred years has been to attain a level of development equivalent to that

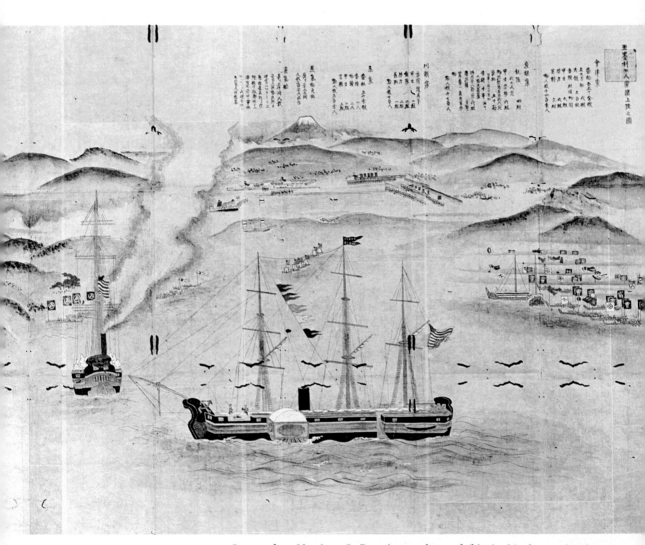

Commodore Matthew C. Perry's squadron of 'black ships' steaming into Kurihama Bay in 1853 on its first visit to Japan. This visit resulted in ending Japan's centuries-long isolation and opening the country to the outside world.

3

The Imperial Palace Plaza and the skyline of Tokyo today.

On April 6, 1868, Emperor Meiji issued the Five Articles of the Imperial Covenant, establishing the fundamentals of national policy. The Emperor is shown listening to the Covenant, being read.

6

of the West and that this rapid rate of growth will continue for the remainder of the present century. He also anticipates that Japan will soon become the world's third largest economy and by the year 2000 will have one of the highest per capita incomes in the world.

Between the Japan seen by Harris and the Japan envisaged by Kahn, the change is indeed staggering.

What, then, has made possible the changes which have occurred in Japan? What were the obstacles that Japan had to overcome to achieve its present status? And, again, what mistakes were made?

It must be obvious that it is difficult to provide complete answers to these questions. Very often, only the barest margin exists between success and failure and so some of the reasons for success can be found in the good fortune with which Japan was blessed. Moreover, as it is often true in human society, so was it true with Japan that too great a success became the cause of subsequent failure.

In looking back over the historical records of the Japanese people at the time of the Meiji Restoration, what strikes us most is that, in the face of a situation fraught with both opportunity and danger, they possessed a determination which carried them with courage and indomitable faith through the vicissitudes of success and failure.

When the Japanese people of today look back with pride over the successful accomplishment of their nation's modernization, they should at the same time be grateful for the good fortune which to a certain degree made this possible.

In any event, the successful achievement of Japan's modernization derives from factors which can be rationally explained. It is to these points that this booklet is addressed.

Two of the first public postal boxes used in 1871 with the inauguration of a modern postal system. The collection time is noted as being at 2:00 p.m.

In January, 1868, opponents to the restoration of Imperial rule were defeated in the Battles of Fushimi and Toba in the outskirts of Kyoto.

The 15th and last Shogun, Yoshinobu Tokugawa, proclaiming his relinquishment of power on November 7, 1867, at Nijo Castle, Kyoto.

CHAPTER TWO

Nationalism

JAPAN'S modernization was carried out to counter the impact of the West. In the nineteenth century, when the influence of European powers moved with increasing momentum toward the East, the Japanese people came to feel that their independence was being threatened. A way of thinking, not in terms of the clan, but in terms of the state, i.e. a national consciousness, was engendered out of this sense of danger. The maintenance of independence thus became, to every Japanese, the most important national purpose. This nationalism enabled the people to transcend the ideological conflicts that cannot be avoided in periods of violent change.

The confrontation between the groups advocating an open-door policy and those advocating the exclusion of foreigners was a bitter one that sharply divided public opinion. It was, however, a confrontation on the question of how best to preserve national independence. Those who were advocating the exclusion of foreigners should not in the least be considered as harbouring a primitive hatred of foreigners; and it was precisely for this reason that they were quick to withdraw their contention when they realized that Japan's independence would not be preserved without opening the nation's doors to modern civilization.

The conflict of views between those who considered that the country should return to the imperial system and those who maintained that the traditional political system, headed by the Shogunate, should be preserved was also a bitter one. However, here again, a common purpose existed, namely, the preservation of Japan's independence.

In both these confrontations, there was a common recognition that if national independence were to be preserved, the divided condition of the nation under numerous feudal overlords must be rectified and a single unified state be brought into being. The only difference of opinion that existed was over the question of which group should prevail in bringing about this unification of the country.

Accordingly, a violent struggle broke out between the Satsuma and Choshu clans and the Shogunate. But both sides saw to it that foreign powers did not get too deeply involved in this domestic struggle. At that time, sharp diplomatic manoeuvering was taking place between Great Britain, supporting the Satsuma and Choshu clans, and France, backing the Shogunate. Depending upon the attitude of the Japanese people, France and Great Britain might well have assumed control of the political situation. However, rather than achieve victory with the help of the French, the Shogunate chose to be overthrown by the Satsuma-Choshu coalition. Consequently, Japan's unification was accomplished with relatively minor confusion. This was because over the 2,000 years of Japanese history, the Emperor had drawn around his person the respect and affection of the Japanese people as the central figure of the spiritual unity of the nation, and the people preferred direct Imperial

Emperor Meiji receiving the Minister of the Netherlands, on March 23, 1868, the first Imperial audience ever granted to foreign envoys.

Two examples of early Meiji school buildings:
(above) Sapporo Clock Tower Building, built in 1878, originally the auditorium of the Sapporo Agricultural College (present-day Hokkaido University);
(below) one of the early primary schools still extant, built in 1876.

rule to intervention by foreign powers.

Sentiment of Loyalty

This spirit of nationalism and this sentiment of loyalty were characteristics of Japan in the Meiji period. Such a psychology was apparent even among those who opposed the Meiji Government. For example, Yukichi Fukuzawa, one of Japan's pioneering educators, expressed his opposition to the tendency toward an increasing governmental predominance by establishing Japan's first private institution of higher learning, Keio University. Yet, even for him, the independence of the state was a matter of highest concern and he sought for this purpose, as an educator, to bring forth men of outstanding character.

Another example is that of Emori Ueki, a leading liberal politician of the Meiji period. While severely criticizing the authoritarian Meiji Government by preaching freedom and equality, he at the same time declared that any person who was unable to extend his own capacity and utilize his own talents was failing in his service to the nation.

Unless given wise direction, this swelling tide of nationalism could have given rise only to emotional stimulation among the Japanese people. Consequently, it is noteworthy that the Meiji Government with firm resolve guided the energies of the nation toward channels that were needed for the urgent task of national construction, difficult though it was. Among the many painful decisions taken by the Meiji Government, three are worthy of particular attention.

Three Painful Decisions

First, the Meiji Government resisted the temptation to unify public opinion through external adventures and preferred to engage in the more steady task of domestic construction. The issue of the invasion of Korea, which arose a mere six years after the establishment of the Meiji Government, was sufficient to split opinion within the Government. It stemmed from the fact that the country was divided at home and plagued by discontented elements; and the advocates of this policy sought to unify public opinion by diverting national attention abroad through an invasion of neighbouring Korea. It was a common device often resorted to by nations in the past. While this could have temporarily unified public opinion, in the long run it would have meant wasting precious national resources and retarding economic construction at home without producing any positive results. For this reason, after heated debate, the Meiji Government rejected the proposal in 1873. Subsequently, the fact that efforts were concentrated on a policy of 'home administration and improvement' became a major turning point in this nation's modern history.

The second painful decision which the Meiji Government had to make was to institute a drastic deflationary policy in 1881. Between 1876 and 1880, Japan experienced a rather severe inflation which substantially reduced the real purchasing power of government revenues. The Government barely managed to avoid a financial crisis by introducing new taxes on wine and tobacco. At the same time, the Government was forced to reduce expenditures for promoting modern industries and other investments. As a result, it became difficult to achieve the targets set by the Government for economic development. It was then that the Meiji Government, with firm resolve, carried out steps needed to halt inflation, such as the re-introduction of convertible currency and other stringent fiscal measures.

Emperor Meiji and his entourage, in splendid procession, entering Tokyo Castle, the new Imperial residence, on November 26, 1868.

(above) Samples of the currency issued by the Meiji Government for nationwide use.
(below) Inaugural ceremonies for the Bank of Japan, April 10, 1896.

As is invariably the case when a deflationary policy is instituted, so it was in Japan that public dissatisfaction was heightened. But, the Meiji leaders remained firm. As a result, inflation was halted in 1884 and the economic goals set in 1868 were achieved by 1885, as planned.

Thirdly, in the procurement of funds necessary for industrialization, the Meiji leaders did not resort to the easy method of attracting foreign investments, but chose to raise the needed funds from within the country by instituting a land tax. These leaders realized, of course, that capital was a vital requirement in the modernization of the nation's industries, but at the same time they feared that by seeking foreign capital Japan might become economically dependent upon foreign countries and thus subservient to their influence. Foreign investments were therefore held down to a minimum. Public bonds, valued at one million pounds sterling, were floated in England with a 9 per cent interest rate to start the railway industry in 1870. Later, in 1873 a further 2-1/4 million pounds sterling, at 7 per cent interest, was successfully raised for salary adjustments of feudal officials. With these two exceptions, there were no external borrowings until the end of the Sino-Japanese War in 1895.

It is, of course, doubtful whether the inflow of foreign capital would really have brought about Japan's economic subservience to foreign interests. Indeed, a reasonable degree of foreign investment might well have accelerated economic development.

Nevertheless, the major portion of capital required for economic construction had to be raised at home. In this sense, the decision of the Meiji leaders to raise capital by collecting a land tax from the farmers, despite their bare subsistence level, was indeed commendable.

In any event, as can be seen in these three examples, if these leaders found certain measures necessary for economic construction, they carried them out however difficult and unpopular they might be. In this way, the energies engendered by a growing sense of nationalism were guided by these leaders with a strong sense of responsibility.

It might be useful to review, at this point, the specific measures which emerged from these three great decisions.

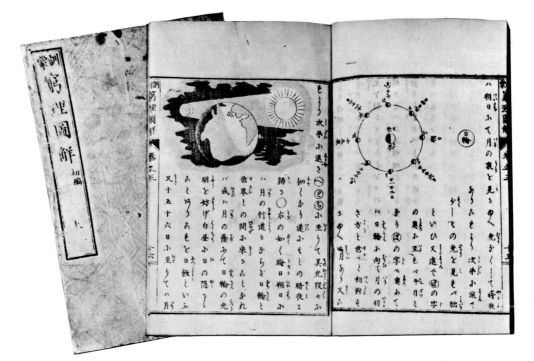

Page of a school textbook, published in 1868, explaining the phases of the moon.

Japan's first foreign mission, headed by Prince Iwakura, Ambassador Extraordinary and Plenipotentiary, leaving Yokohama for the United States and Europe on December 23, 1871.

21

Emperor Meiji tried to encourage his people in all their tasks. Here, he views farmers harvesting the rice crop near Nagoya, in 1868.

CHAPTER THREE

Centralization

THE most important factor in Japan's economic development was a strong and integrated control by the central government.

One of the first steps taken in this connection by the new government was the abolition of the feudal administrative areas of the clans in 1871 and the establishment of prefectures to be administered by governors appointed by the central government. This was no easy task, since it meant that the feudal overlords, who constituted the great landowners of the Tokugawa period, would be deprived of their rights.

The founding fathers of Meiji, nevertheless, were fully aware of the fact that unless feudal decentralization was abolished, the authority of the central government could never be established and that consequently economic development would not take place. 'Rather than fail now, it would be better to fail in the process of carrying out a momentous decision.' Such was the sentiment of the leaders as they resolutely pushed through their policy of centralization.

This step was followed by the establishment of the armed forces, directly under the control of the central government, and thus was the foundation of power for the Meiji Government consolidated.

Better Communications

Parallel with the process of centralization of authority, improvements in the communications system were carried out; railway, telegraphic and postal systems which constituted the arteries and nerves of the state were introduced.

Moreover, the fact that the reading of newspapers was encouraged was important as part of the effort to integrate communications. The Government drastically reduced the postal rates for newspapers and permitted the free mailing of articles and stories by contributors, thus assisting the papers in their news and editorial activities. Furthermore, public reading facilities were established in towns and villages where newspapers were made available, usually free of charge, for those who could not afford to purchase them.

By keeping the people informed of events at home and abroad, these measures contributed immensely toward nurturing in the mind of each individual the sense that he was an integral part of the national entity. The fact that at that time Japan had achieved a standardization of its language and enjoyed a literacy rate exceeding 40 per cent was a great asset.

Another kind of integration that was needed was in the economic field. A new system of weights and measures was established to replace local standards which existed as remnants of the feudal past, the land tax was amended and cadastral surveys carried out. Heretofore, farmers had been measuring their acreage in terms of what the land produced. Henceforth, the more generally valid geometric standards were to be applied.

汐留より蒸気車通行の図

Woodblock print of a station and trains of the first railway line, running between Tokyo and Yokohama. The line was opened in 1872.

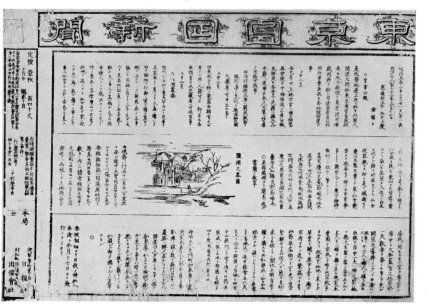

(above) The main office of the Tokyo Nichi-Nichi Newspaper (present-day Mainichi) in 1876. (left) front page of the first issue of the Nichi-Nichi, March 19, 1872.

Since this was something new and strange to the traditional methods of production and the livelihood of the farmer, it resulted in a certain degree of confusion. Nevertheless, it was obvious that these reforms were prerequisites in integrating local economic communities, operating on a small scale, into the larger perspective of the national economy.

Dismantling Feudalism

Of equal importance with integration were the measures taken to free economic activity from feudal restrictions. The Meiji leaders had already perceived with wisdom the fact that progressive economic activities in the nation as a whole were essential in order to make the country strong and wealthy.

At first, the Meiji leaders were impressed only by the military strength of the European powers. They soon began to realize, however, that the weapons used by these foreign powers were not only superior in quality but also were being produced in large quantities, which meant these countries were wealthy and possessed an advanced technology. Thus they came to recognize that in order to make the country wealthy, the nation as a whole had to adopt a progressive attitude toward economic activities.

Eiichi Shibusawa, leading industrial figure of the Meiji period and founding force behind many of Japan's important business concerns, was impressed during his stay in Europe by the fact that the relationships among industrialists, officials and the military were on an equal and horizontal pattern as opposed to the vertical relationships that persisted in Japan. He felt that in a country like Japan, where official authority was predominant, justice could often be thwarted by power. Therefore, Japan had much to learn from Europe in this respect. This attitude was shared by many others of the Meiji leaders.

It was in view of such a consideration that, immediately after its establishment in 1868, the Meiji Government carried out in quick succession a series of measures designed to eliminate feudal restrictions.

In 1868, the system of limited shareholding was abolished, thus removing the restrictions of a monopolistic system derived from feudal guilds. Between 1871 and 1872, the caste system based upon the four classes of society was abolished and the freedom of choice in employment by all classes of people was recognized, thus permitting full play to the creative genius of the nation.

By 1872, the farmers had been given their freedom of choice in selecting what crops they would grow and in selling and purchasing land. Through these measures, agricultural development was promoted.

Education, A Key Factor

The enhancement of social mobility was another step forward.

The abolition of the feudal caste system was aimed at removing the obstacles to such social mobility. Moreover, on the heels of this reform, great efforts were made in the field of education as a result of which able persons were increasingly utilized, thus substantially contributing to social mobility.

In one respect, the Meiji leaders considered that in order to make the country wealthy and strong it was important to raise the intellectual level of the general masses. They realized

Woodblock print of a classroom scene in a 'terakoya,' or private temple school, of the pre-Meiji era.

Yukichi Fukuzawa, pioneering educator and founder of Keio University.

Japan's first public speaking hall, built in 1874 on the campus of Keio University and still in use.

the need of an efficient labour force to start new industries. They knew that in a modern military establishment a reasonably high level of intelligence would be required not only of the officers but of the men as well. That is to say, the general capacity of the individual citizen had to be enhanced.

They considered that, from the standpoint of national integration, education was a basic factor. They established schools throughout the country and sought to disseminate education in order to change Japan fundamentally.

The Japanese people, for their part, did not hesitate to seize the opportunities thus provided. When the government lacked sufficient funds to build primary schools, local landlords helped to establish them by giving large donations for this purpose.

Moreover, since the days of the Tokugawa regime, the people of Japan had been accustomed to attending the 'terakoya' or private temple schools and consequently held education in high regard. Perhaps the greatest legacy inherited by Meiji Japan in its process of modernization was education.

Up to the time of the Meiji Restoration, some 50 per cent of the male population, and 15 per cent of the female population, had been receiving some sort of formal education outside their homes. Consequently, a large number of the merchant and farmer classes as well as the entire warrior class were able to read and write. The fact that there existed such a foundation, in addition to the strong sense of self-improvement, a characteristic of the Japanese people, greatly facilitated the acceptance of the concept of general primary education.

Creating Social Mobility

In this way, national education was disseminated rapidly

so that in the final years of the Meiji period, the rate of primary school attendance exceeded 95 per cent. Moreover, middle and higher education served to attract the more outstanding student, another factor which helped to enhance social mobility.

This was because the Meiji leaders, in disseminating education, adopted a strong policy of equal opportunity for all. It is possible that the fact that they themselves had risen from the lower echelons of the warrior class and consequently had come into political power as a result of a social revolution may have influenced their decision. Be that as it may, advancement along the educational ladder from the primary to the higher schools was based on strict examinations designed to test ability.

In order to draw brilliant students from poorer homes, free education was provided in institutions such as military academies and normal schools for teacher training.

The intellectual appetite of the Japanese people may be counted as one of their virtues and their interest in the unknown is particularly strong. Thus, even during the 250 years when the country was closed to the outside world, the study of western science, primarily in the medical field, was pursued by a certain number of people through Nagasaki, the only city permitted at that time to conduct foreign trade.

In mathematics, although the figures were completely different from those used in the West, great progress was achieved in certain fields, and as early as the 17th century, the theory of differential and integral calculus had already been discovered.

This love of learning of the Japanese people, coupled with an academic level which was extremely advanced, although limited to a narrow sphere, provided the conditions necessary,

The Empress attending the inauguration of a girls' school in 1885. This school today is the Girls' Senior High School of Gakushuin, Tokyo.

33

Famous scientists of the Meiji Era

*Jokichi Takamine (1852-1922),
discovered the adrenalin.*

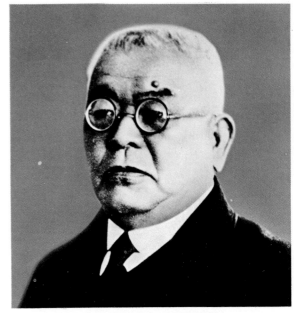

*Shibasaburo Kitazato (1852-1931),
isolated the gangrene bacteria.*

*Kiyoshi Shiga (1870-1957),
isolated the dysentery germ.*

*Hideyo Noguchi (1876-1928),
discovered the spirochete pallida.*

once the Meiji Government introduced Western learning into the country, to bring about an amazing dissemination of general education and to produce scholars who achieved international recognition in various fields of academic endeavour. For example, Dr. Hideyo Noguchi, who was destined to become a world-famous bacteriologist in tropical diseases and who died in the course of his research on yellow fever in Africa, started from humble beginnings as the son of a very poor farmer.

While it is difficult to show by figures the relationship between the objectives of education and social mobility, one aspect of the rapid transition can be seen in the fact that in 1878 some 74 per cent of the students at Tokyo Imperial University came from the aristocracy, or warrior class, and 25 per cent were commoners, whereas by 1885 the corresponding proportions were 52 per cent and 48 per cent respectively, an approximate balance between the two class levels.

In any event, the process of disseminating education and enhancing social mobility was important since it succeeded in drawing out the dynamic power of the nation and further consolidating it by nurturing able citizens, on the one hand, and utilizing them effectively, on the other.

Agricultural implements and tools of the pre-Meiji era.

Emperor Meiji always paid an annual visit to Tokyo Imperial University to attend graduation exercises. The Imperial coach is shown entering the university grounds.

37

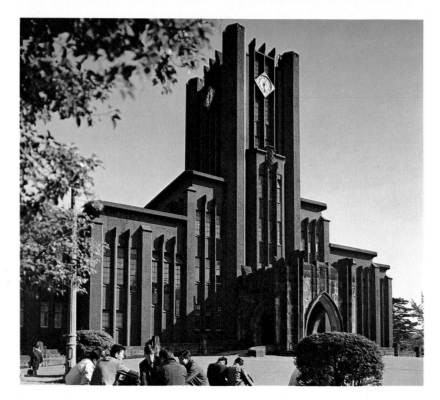

Two views of present-day Tokyo University.

CHAPTER FOUR

Procurement of Capital

A S mentioned earlier, since Japan did not import capital from abroad on a large scale, the construction and development of modern industries in the initial period depended upon the accumulation of capital derived from the traditional sector of the economy, namely, agriculture.

The importance of the agricultural sector is demonstrated clearly in the proportion which the land tax occupied in central and local government revenues in the early years of the Meiji period. It constituted some 72 per cent between 1873 and 1878, and 64 per cent between 1879 and 1883.

Thus, the fact that in the early period of Meiji an accelerated growth occurred in the traditional sector of Japan's economy, including agriculture, was important to the extent that it enabled Japan to launch its programme of economic development.

The first step which allowed the accelerated growth of agriculture was the removal of feudalistic restrictions. Soon after the Meiji Restoration, permanent restrictions on the sale and purchase of land, restrictions on the cultivation of certain types of crops, and other restrictions on movement between communities and on commercial transactions and communications were removed. These steps helped to stimulate technological development.

To take one example, the technological progress which had occurred regionally during the Tokugawa period now extended throughout the land. During the feudal period, improved varieties of high quality seeds were forbidden to be sold to other clans for fear of shortage and, in some cases, such transactions between villages of the same clan were prohibited. With the Meiji Restoration, however, such obstacles were removed and improved seeds were widely disseminated.

Spirit of Enterprise

The fact that agriculture was freed from feudalistic restrictions gave the landowning farmer, who constituted the mainstay of agricultural production up to that time, a new field of activity. It is noteworthy that among these people an entrepreneurial spirit was engendered. In collaboration with others who shared their views, they embarked upon a series of agricultural improvements. For example, an agricultural discussion group, formed in 1874, became Japan's first farm organization.

The first task which farmers undertook was the improvement of the strains of rice. This was the most obvious and immediate task and one that took the least time. They exchanged various types of seeds from different parts of the country and carried out experiments in cross-pollination, which helped to increase production. 'Seed-exchange meetings' were a reflection of these activities and the most well-known of these meetings is the one in Akita Prefecture, which was established in 1878 and continues to this day.

The Empress occasionally visited the rice fields situated within the grounds of the Imperial Palace. Here, she views the transplanting of the young rice plants.

41

Emperor Meiji undertook tours of the various provinces during his reign.
On his tour of the northeastern region in 1876, the local farmers of
Morioka displayed their horses and riding techniques to His Majesty.

With regard to methods of cultivation, progress was made in a similar step-by-step fashion. One was the improvement in the methods of irrigation, while another was broadening the use of fertilizers, which arose in connection with the former development. From feudal times, fertilizers made from herring fish were used to a certain extent in Hokkaido. With the development of transportation between different sections of the country, this practice became widespread. While it was originally confined to cultivating special products, such as cotton, it eventually came to be used in rice cultivation.

Later, soya bean cakes began to be imported from China and these replaced fish fertilizers and were more extensively used.

Role of Government

It was significant that these technical improvements were initiated by the farming population. But the Meiji Government also assisted in fostering this trend. For example, in 1885, the Government established a system whereby it dispatched groups of touring instructors to the countryside. This programme involved the commissioning of working farmers (landowning farmers possessed with the entrepreneurial spirit) who were actively engaged in technical innovations to travel the countryside to impart new methods of cultivation.

Parallel with this system, the Government established a private institute in Fukuoka Prefecture in 1882 for instruction in agricultural management. This institute also dispatched practical instructors throughout the country. As one of its achievements, an improved form of plough-share was introduced. Up to that time, the hand-plough was the only implement available, inhibiting the level of agricultural productivity.

The Government continued, thereafter, to direct agricultural development and established, in 1893, a national agricultural experimental station for improving techniques. A policy of subsidizing agricultural improvement was also instituted.

Modern Industry

Japan's modern industries were built on a foundation created through the development of the traditional sector of the economy. Here again, the Government played a most important role in this development.

The Government granted subsidies to what it considered to be the most promising industries and itself engaged in the management of state enterprises. It was not the intention of the Government, however, to assume for itself the task of industrialization, but rather to foster private entrepreneurship out of the new economic class.

As stated earlier, the Meiji leaders realized that it was the free and unhampered economic activities of the people of Western countries that constituted their real source of power and there were those in Japan who argued that to admit self-interest, as was done in the West, was more in the greater national interest than the futile emphasis on moral considerations indulged in by Asians.

The fact that the Government removed feudal restrictions, such as the monopoly on shareholding, stemmed from the consideration that free and unhampered activity of the people was the key to economic development.

However, in comparison with European countries, Japan was clearly inferior in respect of organization, techniques and capital. The challenge could not be met by liberalization alone.

Woodblock print of a scene at the first National Fair, held in Tokyo, in 1877.

Woodblock prints showing the exterior (above) and the interior (below) of Japan's first spinning factory to apply a mass-production system, opened in 1872.

Moreover, since the Japanese people were as yet unaccustomed to modern industries, it was hardly to be expected that they would naturally proceed to invest in this sector. Furthermore, because of their long association with the feudal period, the Japanese people were more accustomed to protectionist policies than to free enterprise. It was for this reason that the Government was left with no alternative but to play a major role in the development of the country's industries.

Joint-stock Companies

In its function of fostering the country's modern industries, the Government undertook as one of its first steps to assist in the conversion of business organizations into joint-stock companies.

The principle by which joint-stock companies functioned was already known in Japan before the Meiji Restoration. With the establishment of the Meiji Government, full-scale efforts were launched to establish such companies.

By granting special privileges, such as increased subsidies, the Government sought to appeal to the wealthy businessmen to establish foreign-exchange firms, trading companies, transportation companies, and the like. Thus were joint-stock companies established.

During the Tokugawa period, economic activity in Japan was conducted on the principle of the family system and was, by its very nature, wholly different from that of a joint-stock company. For this reason, if the Government had not assisted and encouraged them, joint-stock companies would never have developed as rapidly as they did.

The Government also granted extensive financial assistance

to enterprises breaking new ground. For example, one company was granted several steamships and a large subsidy. At that time, Japan's maritime transportation was being conducted on a very modest scale and international trade was in the hands of foreign shipping companies. The Government sought to build Japan's own shipping companies.

In 1879, to assist the spinning industry, the Government sold 10 spinning machines to a private firm with very easy terms of payment which consisted of a redemption period of over 10 years, interest-free. In 1881, when the Japan Railway Company was established, the company was exempted from any land tax on its own property and, regardless of whether there were any profits or not, was guaranteed an 8 per cent dividend per annum. These are but a few examples.

When the Government deemed that a certain industry or enterprise was necessary to the achievement of the national purpose of economic modernization, and considered that the particular company possessed some degree of strength of its own but could not be expected to stand on its own feet, subsidies were granted to make the enterprise viable.

Government-managed Factories

Another activity by which the Government sought to assist the development of industries involved the building of model factories, directly operated by the Government.

These model factories represented a broad range of industrial production: steel, cement, plateglass, firebrick, woollen textiles and spinning.

While the objective of the individual factory was dependent upon the particular type of production it was engaged in, there were in general three purposes to the Government's policy:

Two 1880 woodblock prints showing industries of the Meiji period:
(above) shipbuilding; (right) clockmaker.

The Yawata Steel Company built Japan's first blast furnace in 1901 (left). In 1970, Yawata merged with the Fuji Steel Company to form the gigantic Nippon Steel Corporation (below: Yawata works in Kyushu).

1) to exhibit the production methods and techniques of European-type factories; 2) to be self-sufficient in the production of new products which hitherto had to be imported from abroad; 3) ultimately to earn a profit. Of these three, the first was the most important. Furthermore, the model factories which the Government built were greatly dependent upon new techniques, and private interests were reluctant to invest in these new types of enterprises. The fact that the Government itself elected to invest in these areas broke the way for others to follow.

Bureaucracy

These policies to promote industry were primarily carried out by officials of the Ministry of Finance, but involved other governmental agencies as well. These were men who were convinced that if national independence were to be preserved, the nation's economic well-being had to be secured.

It was extremely fortunate for Japan that men of this calibre rose to positions of leadership in the few years following the Meiji Restoration. It was they who restrained those who advocated the exclusion of the 'foreign barbarians' or favoured overseas adventures.

They must be given the credit for directing the energies of the nation toward full-scale economic construction in a difficult period.

Toshimichi Okubo, who was typical of this group of leaders, was astounded to see, in his travels in Europe, the enormous gap that existed between European civilization and that of his own country and, thereafter, dedicated his life to the modernization of his country.

The deep-rooted conviction that Japan had to catch up with the West, coupled with an accurate assessment of the facts, became their driving force.

Through such leadership, industries in Japan began their march forward on the road to modernization. This is typically illustrated in the fact that the land tax, which constituted 72 per cent of government revenues in the early Meiji years, had become less than 20 per cent by the end of the Meiji period.

It should be recognized, however, that the assets from the past together with a substantial measure of good fortune contributed to the success of Japan's economic modernization. The fact that already, in the Tokugawa period, the people had become impressed with the importance of commerce, on the one hand, while, on the other, roads and shipping routes had been developed, meant that an economic structure on a nation-wide scale had already come into existence.

In the traditional sector of its economy, Japan possessed ideal commodities for export in the form of silk and tea. The foreign exchange earning power of these goods was absolute and Meiji Japan, in exporting them, was able to procure the material necessary for its industrialization.

The opening of the first session of the Imperial Diet on November 29, 1890, in the presence of the Emperor.

Emperor Meiji promulgating the nation's Constitution on February 11, 1889, in an impressive ceremony at the Imperial Palace.

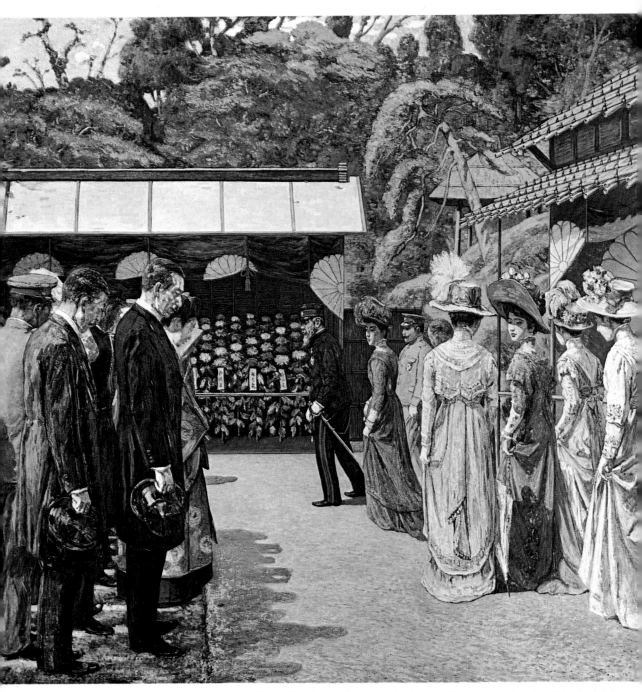

Imperial chrysanthemum-viewing parties at the Akasaka Detached Palace have been annual events since 1880. The Emperor and Empress are shown here at the 1909 garden party.

56

CHAPTER FIVE

Attitude toward the West

WHAT must not be overlooked in reviewing the modernization of Japan is the attitude of the Japanese people toward foreign countries.

As mentioned earlier, the people of the Meiji period were extremely cautious toward the West and consequently did not seek capital from abroad. This did not mean, however, that they allowed themselves to be captured by narrow anti-foreign sentiments toward foreigners and things foreign. They considered that the employment of foreigners for introducing foreign techniques entailed no danger. In fact, they offered high salaries to attract them.

In almost all fields of national activity, such as the legal, military and economic, foreigners were employed. These men were sincere and serious and did not stop at providing only the necessary knowledge but undertook on their own initiative to perform the role of advisors.

Moreover, students were dispatched abroad. They assimilated the advanced knowledge of the Western countries and upon their return to Japan were able to assume positions of leadership.

In this situation, the Japanese people gladly embraced Western culture. 'Civilization and enlightenment' became a fashionable phrase. There was a time in which the people tended to belittle the traditional cultural legacy and to be satisfied with anything, provided it was new. 'Hakuraihin,' or foreign-made products, were sought after and it was the fashion of the day to wear foreign clothes and accessories and to imitate foreign customs.

Various drastic proposals were also suggested after careful consideration. For example, Arinori Mori, who was to become the nation's first Minister of Education, advocated the abolition of Chinese characters in the written language and their replacement by the alphabet.

Meiji Japan thus sought to bring about sudden change in everything. There were, of course, some negative results of this drive, but it cannot be denied that it was this which made possible the introduction of Western culture into Japan.

Confusion of Values

The greatest problem involved in the introduction of Western culture was the confusion of values which occurred. Latent in this process was the danger that the social, cultural and spiritual unity of the country might be destroyed.

Faced with this danger, the intellectual leaders of the late Tokugawa period sought their answer in such formulae as 'Eastern morals and Western art,' 'Japanese spirit and Occidental learning.' In actual fact, however, such formulae were found to be ineffective because a civilization or culture is an indivisible whole and it is impossible to adopt only the scientific or technical aspects of it and exclude the rest.

Prime Minister Katsura announcing to the House of Peers the full text of the Anglo-Japanese Alliance, signed in London in January, 1902.

Two examples of Meiji buildings: (above) the Akasaka Detached Palace; (left) original Imperial Hotel, built 1890.

For this reason, when Western culture was introduced into Japan, it was inevitable that the values of the West should come into conflict with those of the traditional culture. This led to confusion. However, since value patterns are the product of long history, new value patterns could not be easily created with the result that the old attitudes toward life slowly disintegrated.

The eminent novelist, Soseki Natsume, observed that because Japan's modernization had been accomplished in haste, as a result of foreign pressures, the conscience and sincerity of the Japanese people had been lost and a shallow society, filled with deceit, had come into being. He had been following, with some concern and pessimism, the trend of events in Japan after the Russo-Japanese War, but there can be no question that he had an accurate measure of the danger into which Japan was at that time falling.

Nevertheless, the introduction of Western culture into Japan was absolutely essential. And even if the process entailed some confusion in values, there could be no turning back.

The first Japanese-made steam locomotive, built in 1895.

CHAPTER SIX

International Power Struggle

AT about the time that this phenomenon of confusion in values had begun to attract the attention of the Japanese people, Japan was beginning to face difficulties in other areas.

For one thing, the stern realities of international politics were making themselves felt with increasing severity. Until the time of the Sino-Japanese War of 1894-1895, the objective of Japanese diplomacy was clear, limited only to seeking the preservation of national independence. Accordingly, when Japan went to war with China, it had the support of almost every Japanese and the Japanese people rejoiced in the victory.

While victory in the Sino-Japanese War assured the preservation of Japan's independence, it did not mean that Japan's problems in the international arena were over. Quite the contrary, it meant that having become stronger, Japan was forced to become involved in the international power struggle. In the midst of the elation that swept the country over its victory in the Sino-Japanese War, Japan was suddenly confronted with the intervention of three powers, led by Russia.

It is, of course, possible to argue that Japan was not wise in demanding the Liaotung Peninsula as the price of victory.

Nevertheless, Russia's intervention stemmed from purely self-ish motives and this became clear when, soon after the Liao-tung Peninsula had been returned by Japan as a result of the three-power intervention, these three powers, together with Britain, obtained long-term leases of strategic locations from China.

Prior to the three-power intervention, the Japanese people were extolling the West, even while taking a cautious attitude toward it. They thought that if Japan could become a civilized state and join the ranks of the advanced countries of the West, they could hope for peace and tranquility. And just as this objective appeared to be within reach, the Japanese people were made to realize that a bitter struggle was taking place among the great powers of the world.

At the time of the Sino-Japanese conflict, wartime songs were on a gay note, taking as their theme, for example, that progress will overcome the decadent past. In contrast, the songs of the Russo-Japanese War of 1904-05 were sombre and sad in tone. This typified, perhaps, the beginning of the hard struggle that Japan was to face in international power politics.

Agricultural Stagnation

At about this time, Japan was facing increasing obstacles at home. That is to say, in the traditional sectors of the economy, such as agriculture, which had been an important pillar in sustaining the country's economic modernization, the rate of growth had begun to drop.

In the first place, Japan had always suffered from a shortage of arable land and a high density of population. As Japan's agriculture began to develop through the traditional methods, it came face to face with this problem of the shortage of land. As a result, marginal lands had to be brought under

The Battle of the Yellow Sea during the Sino-Japanese War (September 17, 1894).

Entry of the Japanese Army into Mukden, Manchuria, during the Russo-Japanese War (March 15, 1905).

66

cultivation with a consequent rise in costs, resulting in a slowdown in the increase rate of production.

Theoretically, it was possible to develop agricultural production at the same fast rate as before by using improved agricultural techniques. In other words, improvements were possible in such fields as seeds and saplings, fertilizers, irrigation, drainage and agricultural machinery. As for seeds and saplings and fertilizers, technical improvements were relatively easy. However, improvements involving land and capital could not be carried out on a small scale.

Farm lands were subdivided into small lots and holdings were on a small scale, with the result that capital and land improvements were not made. Investments for these purposes were too costly for most landowners.

Furthermore, there was still an abundant supply of cheap labour in the villages. With the rapid economic growth in Japan, there was a huge outflow of labour from the villages into the towns and modern industrial areas. Nevertheless, the absolute number of agricultural workers showed practically no change from 1868 to 1930. Consequently, as far as the landowners were concerned, it was easier for them to depend upon the cheap labour that existed in abundance, rather than to raise productivity through expensive investments.

Burden of Military Expense

The policies of the Government were, to a certain extent, responsible for this agricultural stagnation.

From the Meiji period onward, Japan's military expenditure was enormous and soon came to represent 10 per cent of the national income, with the result that investments in industry were reduced. It was, of course, difficult to estimate the military capacity required to preserve Japan's independence. Nevertheless, in spite of the fact that Japan was considerably poorer than European countries, it sought to catch up with them militarily. As a result, Japan became a strong military power out of proportion to its economic capacity and had to bear the consequent financial burden.

A certain economist has observed that if Japan had been able to avoid the Sino-Japanese and Russo-Japanese wars, it could have reduced its military expenditure by half, making possible, through this reduction in expenditure, a considerable reduction in the land tax and an increase in disbursements for economic purposes, particularly agriculture. He noted also that by further assistance to industry, coupled with a greater encouragement to agriculture, the growth rate during the Meiji period would have been considerably higher than it actually was. What was more important, he claimed, was the fact that if this had been done, it would have been possible to offset the unrest and tension of the agrarian communities which eventually led the country toward the path of militarism.

This would certainly have been difficult but would appear, nonetheless, to have been the wiser course.

The First World War

Another circumstance was, in part, responsible for this agricultural stagnation. The Japanese economy had long been plagued by a chronic imbalance in its international payments. This was perhaps inevitable in the case where a country like Japan, with scarce natural resources, underwent sudden economic development. It is certain that this became a major pitfall for Japan's economy.

Woodblock print of the Yokohama waterfront in 1870.

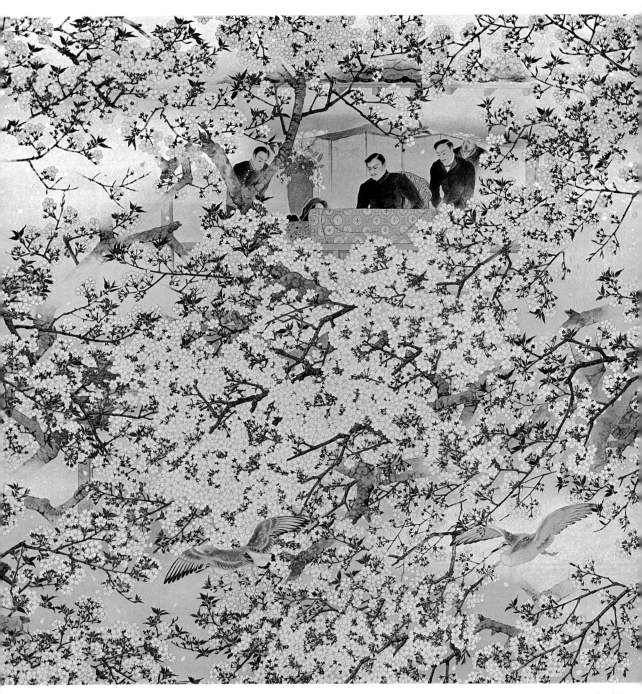

Emperor Meiji viewing cherry blossoms during the early years of his reign.

In more specific terms, the Japanese economy experienced an unprecedented prosperity during the First World War. The disequilibrium in the balance of payments disappeared and exports rose sharply. However, in the face of this sudden boom, the Government was without an adequate financial policy which contributed, in part, to bringing about inflation. A considerable part of the nation suffered a drop in real income.

With the end of the First World War, exports declined sharply and the terms of trade deteriorated. After a swift inflation, Japan experienced over a sustained period a fall in commodity prices. Thus, in order to survive, the modern industries had to adopt rationalization measures which meant raising productivity by bringing in modern techniques, that is to say, making large investments.

Dual Economic Structure

This process of rationalization, however, did not take place in the traditional sector of the economy. The result was that while productivity and capital investment rose in the modern industries, through this rationalization, productivity and wages in the traditional sector remained stagnant, thus creating a large gap between the two.

The most typical example was found in the difference between the workers employed in the modern industries in the cities and the farmers.

In the traditional sector other than agriculture, wages also remained low, thus creating another unfortunate class of people. In this way, a broad division developed in the Japanese economy.

It prevented the continued expansion of the domestic

market and thereby distorted economic growth.

Those who were forced to accept lower standards of living became envious and antagonistic toward those who could afford to lead a more privileged and modern way of life.

The dissatisfaction of these people, particularly the farmers, coupled with the confusion in social values, created the conditions which later led the Japanese people to turn to an extreme ideology. The fact that the people were uneasy in the turbulent international environment caused them to look in an exclusionist direction.

Moreover, the fact that from the 1920's on no outstanding leaders were to be found meant that the Government, instead of directly attacking the problem of domestic dissatisfaction, chose the easy method of directing the people's eyes toward foreign adventures.

Woodblock print of a Tokyo street scene in 1874. To the left and right are department stores of that day and in the centre is the main office of the Mitsui Bank.

東京銀座通電燈建設之圖

An 1883 woodblock print showing the first electric street light on Tokyo's Ginza Street (above) and a view of Shimbashi (left).

Aerial view of central Tokyo at the time of surrender, August, 1945.

Surrender ceremonies on board the U.S.S. Missouri, September 2, 1945.

77

Shigeru Yoshida, then Prime Minister, signing the Treaty of Peace at San Francisco, September 8, 1951.

CHAPTER SEVEN

The Postwar Phase

THE reckless war that ended in 1945 brought great destruction to Japan. Most of its cities were burnt, industries laid waste and food, necessary to sustain life, was in short supply.

The Japanese Government, before rehabilitating the nation's economy, which was in a state of almost complete disintegration, had to start by giving food to the people. The inflation which had been caused by the reckless issue of notes during the war was also a great problem.

Occupation Reforms

However, defeat in war provided, at the same time, the opportunity for national resurgence.

Seeking to change Japan's social structure, the occupation authorities carried out various reforms which, in their ultimate effect, produced organizational changes facilitating subsequent economic growth. Particularly important were the land reforms. Before the Second World War, the slowing down of the rate of agricultural growth was a major problem; the cause was found to lie not in technical but structural defects. For this reason, it is particularly noteworthy that when the tenant-farmer obtained his own land, through land reform, his desire to produce increased.

Moreover, in the process of inflation, wealth which had been concentrated in the cities was re-distributed to the countryside. This, coupled with the dissemination of agricultural cooperatives and the use of new techniques introduced after the war such as insecticides, agricultural chemicals and mechanized implements, helped to raise production.

The parallel growth of industrial and agricultural productivity is a desirable condition for economic growth and this condition obtained in Japan after the Second World War.

The number of agricultural workers dropped sharply from 45 per cent in 1950 to 19 per cent in 1967 and in some cases there was a drop in the absolute number of farm workers in response to the demand for labour in urban areas. Even under such conditions, it was a remarkable achievement that agricultural production could be increased by an average of 2.4 per cent per year.

In this connection, it was particularly important that the problem of land reform had been under study and measures prepared in Japan even before the occupation. However good a programme might be, if it is imposed from the outside, it does not always work. As far as agriculture in Japan was concerned, studies on land reform in order to raise productivity had already been begun before the war, thorough surveys of actual conditions had been made and plans based on such surveys had been worked out.

These preparations made the land reforms compatible with the actual conditions in Japan and contributed greatly to making the programme a success.

The modernization of agriculture has taken rapid strides and mechanized equipment is extensively used today.

Night view of the National Diet Building, focal point of Japan's democratic political system.

Japan's two Nobel Prize winners in the field of physics:
(left) Dr. Hideki Yukawa, recipient in 1949;
(right) Dr. Sin-itiro Tomonaga, recipient in 1965.

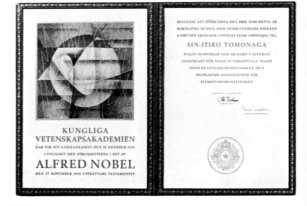

Moreover, agricultural land reform, together with the growth of labour unions and the dissolution of the 'zaibatsu' (great financial trusts), helped to equalize the distribution of wealth and thus to broaden Japan's economic foundation. In other words, it expanded the domestic market and thereby made further industrialization possible.

In postwar Japan, goods were first produced and sold in large quantities on the domestic market, through which process costs were reduced and the same products then exported abroad. Before the war, as was true in the case of cotton, in order to remain competitive on the export market, costs were reduced through low wages. Thus, the situation in the postwar period had been completely altered.

Rehabilitating the Economy

On the basis of these structural reforms, the modern sector of the economy achieved remarkable development.

To rectify the temporary setbacks caused by war and devastation was relatively easy after the temporary period of confusion following the war had passed. All that was needed to be done was to profit from the experience of the advanced countries in economic development and to act accordingly.

Moreover, while the wartime destruction of Japan was a physical one, the most important aspect of the Japanese people, namely the capacity of the individual, remained intact.

As stated before, Japan, historically, had expended much effort on educational development and it was an extremely important advantage for Japan that, because of this circumstance, there existed at that time a highly competent and abundant labour force.

When a quality labour force of this kind is given capital, it is only natural that production should rise rapidly.

In postwar Japan, an infinitely higher proportion, in comparison to foreign countries, of the annual production of goods was directed toward capital accumulation. In 1962, the proportion occupied by total fixed assets in the gross national product was 16.0 per cent in the United States, 19.6 per cent in France, 25.3 per cent in Germany and 34.4 per cent in Japan.

What made this possible was the high propensity to save on the part of the Japanese people, their strong will to invest and numerous investment opportunities, as well as the enlightened interest policy taken by the Government.

This capital, coupled with the new technology introduced from abroad on a large scale after the war, contributed to increasing production. During the period of tension before and during the war, very little technology of the advanced industrial nations was imported into Japan, whereas the postwar period witnessed a major influx, followed by a worldwide development in all kinds of new technology. As a result, not merely was production capacity enhanced, but a retrenchment in imports became possible in such items as cotton and natural rubber, and the degree of dependence on imports did not rise.

Moreover, the introduction of this new technology provided new investment opportunities and had the effect of further promoting capital accumulation.

It is significant that, with the rise in production, Japan's exports increased steadily. Particularly for a country like Japan, which depends upon raw materials from abroad, the expansion of its export trade is a matter of critical importance. Assisted by the general expansion of world trade, Japanese exports increased at a rate higher than that of world trade. As against

Extensive facilities, advanced technology and constant research have brought Japan's iron and steel industry to the third-ranking position in the world.

Night view of a major plant of the petrochemical industry in Chiba Prefecture. The industry enjoys second place in the world today.

The shipbuilding industry has entered the age of mammoth tankers and Japanese yards are constructing ships of the 300,000-ton class.

the 41 per cent increase of world exports during the five-year period between 1958 and 1963, Japan recorded a 100 per cent increase, and its degree of dependence on imports during the period remained stable.

The Role of the Government

In connection with the nation's significant economic growth, the successive postwar governments did not perform as large a role as the Meiji Government. However, when inflation became acute in 1948, the Government resolutely carried out a deflationary policy in the interest of economic rehabilitation, although well aware that this could give rise to public dissatisfaction.

Moreover, as a result of having adopted, in the postwar period, a foreign policy based on international cooperation and dedication to peace, the Government was able to hold down its defence expenditures to a minimum, in comparison with the prewar period. Consequently, investment of capital in the production sector increased remarkably, thus stimulating economic development at an accelerated pace. Furthermore, during the difficult postwar years, the Government sought to give to the nation's economy the capacity to survive in the stringent economic environment that could be expected in the future. To this end, it indicated the direction that the nation would be expected to follow.

Just as in the Meiji period, when it was the government officials who contributed so greatly to the promotion of modernization, so it was in the postwar period that the officials entrusted with the framing of economic policies played the role of helmsmen in guiding the country toward economic development.

One of their most significant achievements was to have planned the sophistication of Japan's industrial structure and to have swiftly carried it out in the 1950's. They decided in the early 1950's that the emphasis in the nation's export trade should be shifted from light industrial products, which still occupied half of total exports, to heavy industrial and chemical products. Having made careful plans to accomplish this shift, they proceeded to execute them.

Where there is an economic level of $300 per capita income, there is a matching industrial structure to sustain it; where there is a $1,000 per capita income, there is also a matching industrial structure to sustain it. The fact that Japan's economy was able to accomplish this transition from one level to the other in a limited space of years is another illustration of its high rate of economic growth.

Good Fortune

This amazing economic recovery and development by Japan was, in part, helped by good fortune.

With the worldwide technological innovations of the postwar period, the appearance of synthetic products reduced the importance of raw materials, as can be seen in the case of natural rubber. Moreover, with the large-scale exploitation of underground resources, the position of the buyer was strengthened and the fact that Japan is a small island country now became an advantage with domestic transportation facilities greatly expanded. With the increasing use of mammoth vessels, maritime transportation has a clear advantage over land-based systems.

Although it was considered a handicap before the war, for

Modern motorways and taller buildings symbolize the urbanization of Japanese cities today.

The Japanese motor vehicle industry also ranks second in the world.

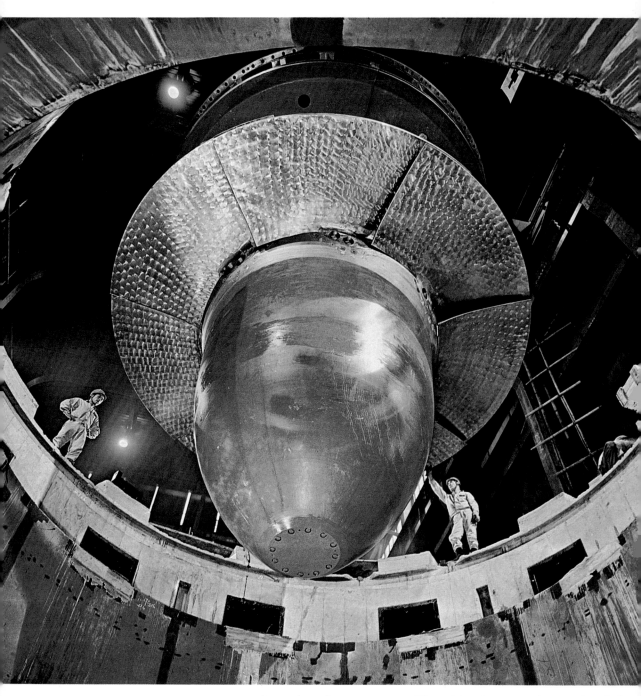

This runner for a 100,000 KW turbine is a typical example of the productive capacity of the nation's heavy industries.

a nation such as Japan to be confined to a small land area, burdened with a large population and poorly endowed with natural resources, this has become no longer true today. This is, indeed, Japan's good fortune.

Lessons from the Past

When the people of Meiji were confronted with a strange and vigorous foreign civilization, they sought it eagerly and, once having accepted it, skillfully adapted it to their own environment.

Again, when confronted with the unprecedented fact of defeat in the Second World War, they persevered and succeeded in the task of national reconstruction to a degree perhaps unknown in the history of the world.

As in the case with human life, a nation must also face many vicissitudes. It is likely in the future that Japan will face her share of difficulties. However, in looking back upon the history of these past one hundred years of modernization, the Japanese people can find the confidence needed in the years ahead, for, in moments of crisis, they have never despaired in their innermost thoughts and have resolutely faced any challenge with determination and dedicated efforts supported by a spirit of self-reliance and steadfast independence.

The enterprising character of the Japanese people, their ability to adapt, and their firm resolve in the face of great challenge: in these qualities lies the key to Japan's century of modernization.

Their Majesties the Emperor and Empress and their family at the Imperial Palace on New Year's Day, 1973.

Schooling today: smock-clad children in kindergarten.

Junior high school geometry class using a teaching machine.

Scenes from the life of a middle-class family of Tokyo.

Modern department stores are found in all major cities today.

The Tea Ceremony, a required social accomplishment for all young ladies.

A super-express train of the New Tokaido Line.

Chronological Outline of Modern Japanese History

Edo Period (1603–1867)

1603 — Tokugawa Ieyasu was appointed Shogun by the Emperor and established his goverment in Edo, present-day Tokyo.

1639 — A ban was placed on the exit of Japanese from, and the entry of foreigners into Japan. Only Protestant Dutch and the non-Christian Chinese were allowed to continue trading at the port of Nagasaki.

1792 — A Russian envoy came to Hokkaido, requesting the opening of trade relations. The Shogunate turned down the request and strengthened the nation's coastal defenses.

1853 — United States Commodore Matthew Perry arrived at Uraga in present-day Kanagawa Prefecture. This visit and the subsequent one in 1854 ended Japan's state of isolation. With the second visit, the Shogunate concluded a Treaty of Amity with the United States, thereby permitting American vessels to stop at two designated ports. This was followed by similar treaties with England, Russia, and the Netherlands.

1856 — Townsend Harris arrived in Shimoda as the first consul general of the United States in Japan.

1867 — The 15th Tokugawa Shogun returned national rule to the Imperial Throne, ending the Tokugawa Shogunate and the rule of warrior government which had started towards the end of the 13th century.

Meiji Period (1868–1912)

1868 — With the restoration of Imperial rule, Emperor Meiji issued an order establishing a new officialdom and proclaiming the direct rule of the Throne in every line of national government.

—Emperor Meiji issued a five-point oath, laying emphasis on respecting public opinion, developing relations with foreign countries and seeking knowledge far and wide.

—Edo was renamed Tokyo, and fixed as the national capital.

—Emperor Meiji arrived in Tokyo to establish the Imperial residence in the new capital.

1869 —The feudal lords returned their domains and people to the Throne.

1870 —The feudal caste system of warrior, farmer, artisan and merchant was abolished.

—Japan's first public bonds, valued at one million pounds sterling, were floated in England with 9 per cent interest to start a railway.

1871 —The modern postal system was inaugurated.

—A currency for nationwide use was issued by the Meiji Government.

—The administrative districts based on the former feudal domains were abolished and the country was divided into prefectures, each with a governor appointed by the central government.

1872 —Farmers were given their freedom of choice in selecting crops and in selling or purchasing land.

—Public primary schools were established throughout the land.

—Japan's first railway, which ran between Tokyo and Yokohama, was opened to traffic.

—The first domestically-made warship "Soryu-maru" was built at Yokosuka Shipyard.

—The Government established four national banks in Tokyo and other cities, and also established the first modern spinning mill in Tomioka, Gumma Prefecture.

1873 —A new system of weights and measures was established to replace local standards.

1874 —The first gaslights were installed along the Ginza street—main street in Tokyo.

1875 —The Meiji Government established the Supreme Court, thereby setting up the new juridical system.

1877 —The first National Fair was held in Tokyo.

1878 —The Tokyo Stock Exchange was opened.

1881 —The Japan Railway Company (first private railway company) was established.
1882 —The Bank of Japan, the nation's central banking institution, was founded.
1887 —Electric lights appeared in Tokyo for the first time.
1889 —The Meiji Constitution was promulgated and limited suffrage introduced.
1890 —The first session of the national parliament was inaugurated, giving the nation the form of constitutional government.
1894 —The Treaty of Commerce and Navigation with Great Britain was signed. Thus was brought to a conclusion the lengthy series of negotiations for the revision of the unequal treaties entered into by the Tokugawa Shogunate.
—Conflicting interests in Korea led to the outbreak of the Sino-Japanese War.
1895 —The war with China ended in victory for Japan.
—Electric trolleys began to run on the streets of Tokyo.
1896 —Motion pictures came to Japan.
1899 —Telephones came into use in Tokyo and Osaka.
1902 —The Anglo-Japanese Alliance was concluded.
1904 —Opposing the advance of Russian influence into Korea, Japan declared war on Russia.
1905 —Japan emerged victorious in the Russo-Japanese War.
1910 —Japan annexed Korea.
1912 —Emperor Meiji passed away.

Taisho Period (1912–1926)

1912 —Emperor Taisho acceded to the Imperial Throne.
1914 —World War I broke out and Japan entered the war on the side of the Allies.
1918 —Commodity prices started to rise, and groups of people who were suffering from the high price of rice staged riots.
1919 —The Versailles Treaty was concluded, with Japan as one of the Allied signatories.
1920 —Japan joined the League of Nations.

1921 — Japan participated in the disarmament conference at Washington, D.C.
1923 — Tokyo was hit by a major earthquake.
1925 — Universal suffrage for adult males was adopted.

Showa Period (1926—   )

1926 — Emperor Taisho passed away and was succeeded by the present Emperor. The name Showa was given to the new era.
1927 — Japan's first subway was opened in Tokyo.
1929 — Japan's first passenger airplane service, between Tokyo and Osaka, was inaugurated.
1930 — Japan participated in the London Disarmament Conference.
1931 — The Manchurian Incident, which led to the Japanese domination of Manchuria, broke out.
1933 — Japan withdrew from the League of Nations, in protest against the League's opposition to Japan's action in Manchuria.
1937 — With increasing military interference and control in politics, Japan started large-scale military operations in China.
1940 — Japan concluded an alliance with Germany and Italy, making her one of the Rome-Berlin-Tokyo Axis Powers.
1941 — Japan launched hostilities against the United States and Great Britain, thus entering World War II.
1945 — Japan surrendered unconditionally to the Allied Powers on the basis of the Potsdam Declaration. Japanese military forces were demobilized, and a program of thorough democratization was instituted.
1946 — The new Constitution was adopted, and universal suffrage was extended to women.
1949 — The Nobel Prize for Physics was awarded to Dr. Hideki Yukawa.
1950 — With the outbreak of hostilities in Korea, the Supreme Commander of the Allied Powers in Tokyo instructed the Japanese Government to set up a National Police Reserve and to increase the strength of the Maritime Safety Agency, the embryo of the present Self-Defense Forces.
1951 — Japan signed a peace treaty at San Francisco with the United

States and almost all of the other Allied Powers.

—The Mutual Security Treaty between Japan and the United States was concluded.

1952 —The San Francisco Peace Treaty came into force, and the Allied occupation ended, restoring full independence to Japan.

1953 —Television broadcasting began in Japan.

1956 —Japan's diplomatic relations with the Soviet Union were restored, with a Joint Declaration terminating the state of war between the two nations.

—Japan was admitted to membership in the United Nations.

1960 —The Mutual Security Treaty between Japan and the United States was amended.

—Japan became the second country in the world after the United States to start regular color television broadcasts.

1964 —The 18th Olympic Games were held in Tokyo.

—The New Tokaido Line, providing superexpress rail service between Tokyo and Osaka, was opened.

—Japan's first expressway, "Meishin," covering the 190-kilometer distance between Kobe and Nagoya, was opened to traffic.

—A commercial monorail transport system was completed in Tokyo.

1965 —The Treaty on Basic Relations between Japan and the Republic of Korea was signed.

—The Nobel Prize for Physics was awarded to Dr. Sin-itiro Tomonaga.

1968 —The Ogasawara Islands were returned to Japan.

—The Nobel Prize for Literature was awarded to Yasunari Kawabata.

—Ceremonies for the Meiji Centenary, marking the 100th anniversary of the start of the Meiji Era, were held throughout the country.

1970 —Expo '70 was held in Osaka.

1972 —The Winter Olympic Games were held in Sapporo.

—Okinawa was returned to Japan.

—Japan's relations with the People's Republic of China were normalized.